IN-COUNTRY

Memories of a Tour of Duty in South Vietnam

By Phillip B. Fehrenbacher

Special thanks to my wife Julie,
for her support in this endeavor,
and putting up with me for 45 years!

Printed by CreateSpace, An Amazon.com Company

This book is dedicated to the men and women of the US military, and our allies who participated in the Vietnam War. Those fortunate enough to survive this hostile environment unfortunately returned home to more turbulance. Nearly 50 years after this experience, I would like to say

"Welcome Home!"

IN-COUNTRY

JUST WHEN YOU THOUGHT **THIS** DETAIL COULDN'T BE WORSE!

IN-COUNTRY

THE 1,000-YARD MEETS THE TWO-YARD STARE!

IN-COUNTRY

THE ROUND PEG IN THE ROUND HOLE!

IN-COUNTRY

WELCOME TO SAIGON, "PEARL OF THE ORIENT!"

IN-COUNTRY

RUMOR HAD IT, IT ONLY TOOK TWO OF THEM TO ROLL UP A MOSQUITO NET...(IF YOU HAD ONE)!

IN-COUNTRY

"JOHN WAYNE" TO THE RESCUE!

IN-COUNTRY

OPINIONS VARIED!

One of the dirtiest, most dangerous jobs in Vietnam was that of being a "Tunnel Rat!" I was never so glad to be 6' 2" and over 200 pounds!

IN-COUNTRY

THE NATURAL!

THE (NOT SO GREAT) WALL OF INDOCHINA.

IN-COUNTRY

MPC...MOUNTAINOUS POCKET CHANGE!

Pardon the lack of radio procedure. Non-military readers may not recognize using numerical representatives for key personnel.

IN-COUNTRY

Just remember what two words sympathy falls between in the dictionary!

IN-COUNTRY

IN-COUNTRY

IN-COUNTRY

This would probably be a lot funnier the next day!

IN-COUNTRY

ANIMAL, VEGETABLE OR MINERAL?
YOU HAVE ALL NIGHT TO DECIDE...

IN-COUNTRY

It was always entertaining to hear non-English speaking bands play popular US songs.

IN-COUNTRY

EM CLUBS SPARED NO EXPENSE TO BRING YOU A LITTLE SLICE OF HOME!

IN-COUNTRY

IN-COUNTRY

**IN-COUNTRY EDUCATION:
INTRODUCTION TO NUOC MAM 101.**

Our malaria pill day was Monday. Proper etiquette was to open mouth and flip pill over right shoulder (careful to miss person in formation behind you).

IN-COUNTRY

MALARIA PILL MONDAY... DO YA FEEL LUCKY?

IN-COUNTRY

REALIZING THE "THRILL" OF COMMAND!

IN-COUNTRY

Pets and mascots varied greatly between units and were popular with MOST guys. We had one dog in our compound (Bullet) and one of the men kept a snake (python?) in his footlocker.

IN-COUNTRY

Viking...Caribbean...Norwegian............eat your hearts out!

IN-COUNTRY

THE SAIGON RIVER CRUISE LINE.

I realize MANY experienced HELL in Vietnam, but for some reason, this particular item really irritates me, and is the cheesiest souvenir I ever saw!

IN-COUNTRY

THE SANDBAG DETAIL
(SOME OF "US" WERE DOING BETTER THAN OTHERS!)

IN-COUNTRY

"ROOMIES!"

Vietnamese kids could ride, pull the buffalo's tail, or anything else without disturbing the animal. I seem to remember guys tell me the buffalo weren't so fond of Americans.

IN-COUNTRY

EAST MEETS WEST!

IN-COUNTRY

AT LEAST THE RED CROSS **ASKED**
IF THEY COULD HAVE YOUR BLOOD!

IN-COUNTRY

END OF THE LINE...MAKE IT HAPPEN!
(S_ _T ROLLS DOWNHILL!)

My second year in country I was fortunate enough to be stationed in Saigon, and occasionally forced to beat cleats back to the compound before curfew. The "Cowboys" could usually get you back in time, but what a ride!

IN-COUNTRY

THE LATE NIGHT DASH FOR CASH!

I never really had any interaction with the "White Mice" (National Police), but there seemed to be one on every corner...until they didn't want to be there.

IN-COUNTRY

SOUTH VIETNAM'S DAVID COPPERFIELD
NOW YOU SEE HIM...NOW YOU DON'T!

The "Saigon Tea." Exorbitantly high-priced non-alcoholic drinks customers bought the bar girls for their company. The girls split the money with the bar, and would stay as long as drinks kept coming.

IN-COUNTRY

LEARNING CONVERSATIONAL VIETNAMESE.

This happened to our unit while calling for air support, during Tet 1968. Fortunately, the officer was asked for confirmation and a tragedy was averted. From then on the Lt was nicknamed "Airstrike," and whenever he appeared at a function somone would shout out "Give me an A...give me an I...give me an R............"

IN-COUNTRY

The Military Payment Certificates (MPC or funny money) was occasionally changed to save MPC being in the hands of Vietnamese business owners and the enemy illegally. Ideally, we were supposed to exchange our MPC for Piasters. Unannounced, military facilities locked their gates and would not let anyone in or out until the exchange was made. After that, the replaced MPC was worthless...lotsa wailing going on!

IN-COUNTRY

THE "SURPRISE" CURRENCY EXCHANGE.

IN-COUNTRY

Sometimes hootch maids/mamasans made themselves a little too much at home! BTW...Crest does not remove betel nut stain.

IN-COUNTRY

MI CASA ES EU CASA?

Every time we had enemy activity in the neighborhood the medics would follow up with a bunch of injections. After nearly two years in Vietnam and a total of four in the Army, I had three to four shot cards filled up on both sides and folded up.

IN-COUNTRY

Military Auxiliary Radio System (MARS) provided phone patches from in-country military to people outside of Vietnam. Your name was placed on a list and maybe (or not) they would make contact sometime that day/night for a 5-minute call. I usually tried when I had all night Charge of Quarters duty. The only down side was that radio operators needed to listen to everything so they could change direction of the conversation when they heard "over."

IN-COUNTRY

THE MARS PHONE CALL
AT&T FOR THE VIETNAM VET!

I hope my more sensitive friends will forgive my wording here. None of the other ideas I considered carried the impact I wanted. This was inspired by the many spiders with palm-sized bodies I saw in our area.

IN-COUNTRY

WELCOME TO THE BUSH!

IN-COUNTRY

NOBODY WANTS TO BE AROUND A SHORTIMER!

Those of us fortunate enough to have gone air transport should remember the feeling of the air sucked out of your lungs when the door was thrown open. The unfortunates on ship transports aclimated to the climate more slowly before reaching land.

IN-COUNTRY

THE FIRST OF **MANY** UNDERSTATEMENTS!

Some guys were experts at land navigation...others, well...NOT!

IN-COUNTRY

WHERE'S A GAS STATION WHEN YOU NEED ONE?

Some infantry units ran orientation schools educating replacements in jungle warfare. One demonstration displayed the ease that a VC "Sapper" could infiltrate perimeter defenses. Under the Hồi Chánh Viên and Chieu Hoi programs enemy defectors aided our training, with many becoming Kit Carson scouts.

IN-COUNTRY

IN-COUNTRY

Not a very funny cartoon today, but I couldn't leave Agent Orange out since nearly all Viet Vets are experiencing it's effects to some degree! The Vietnamese people have also suffered greatly.

IN-COUNTRY

IN-COUNTRY

WHY DON'T YOU DROP IN...AND STAY AWHILE?

I went through the customs process twice, and it seemed like it took about 4 hours to complete for each flight. They gave everyone the chance to dump their contraband without penalties, but usually at least one person was hauled off trying to beat the odds.

IN-COUNTRY

Some military (lucky enough to be in earshot of AFVN radio) were caught up with the exploits of Chickenman!

IN-COUNTRY

WWII HAD CAPTAIN AMERICA...
VIETNAM HAD *CHICKENMAN!*

IN-COUNTRY

SOME TOOK A BIT LONGER TO ADJUST!

MAIL CALL...HIGHLIGHT OF THE DAY!

IN-COUNTRY

ONE MAN'S TRASH IS ANOTHER MAN'S TREASURE!

Everyone remembers how they felt when the wheels lifted for the trip home. The Freedom Bird! The crew ran games like this and the men pinned tons of unit crests, insignia on all the flight attendants...I didn't even mind losing the five bucks!

IN-COUNTRY

ALL RIDING THE "FREEDOM BIRD" WERE WINNERS!

The CO called me in several times to witness a soldier refusing to obey a direct order. One refused and was eventually placed in the Long Binh Jail, or the LBJ Ranch as it was better known. Many didn't realize going there was classified as "bad-time" and did not count off of their tour of duty...they came out with as many days to serve in Vietnam as they had when they entered.

IN-COUNTRY

ANSWER:
NO, AN ALL-EXPENSE PAID TRIP TO THE LBJ RANCH!

IN-COUNTRY

GONE "NATIVE!"

Yeah, this has been done before, but I need to include it with the experience. After nearly two tours I was out-processed and back home playing basketball in a neighborhood gym. A couple of acquaintances asked "Where've you been lately?"

IN-COUNTRY

WELCOME HOME!

The amount of gear guys carried through paddies, up and down hills and mountains in tropical extremes was pretty unbelievable!

IN-COUNTRY

IN-COUNTRY

THE TRANSITION INTO THE MONSOON SEASON.

One of the most sacrosanct possessions of someone in Vietnam was his Short-timer's calendar. 365 numbered days on a chart, helmet cover, or elaborate design (such as a pin-up) were religiously crossed off daily to show how many days were left before returning to the Land of the Big PX!

IN-COUNTRY

HAVING YOUR WHOLE YEAR....."WIPED OUT!"

IN-COUNTRY

TET 1968:
WHEN NEARLY EVERYONE WAS IN THE INFANTRY!

Ohh yeah...The Paris Peace Talks...zzzzzzzzzzzzzzzzzzzz!

NOT GOING ANYWHERE FOR A WHILE?
(APOLOGIES TO SNICKERS)

I think some of my friends could sniff out a cupcake hidden in a full cargo plane before a drug-sniffing dog could locate a pallet of heroin on a landing strip!

IN-COUNTRY

**SHARING YOUR CARE PACKAGE FROM HOME
WITH YOUR..."BUDDIES!"**

Not all "Tops" were this bad, but I had more than my share of them!

IN-COUNTRY

The Vietnamese were among the most resourceful, innovative people I ever met. I saw an attractive golden foot locker one day, when I opened it up I was looking at the printed side of many flattened beer cans. When the Vietnamese threw something away, there was absolutely no possible use for it!

IN-COUNTRY

GENUINE WAR SOUVENIRS...WHILE YOU WAIT!

I took a 30 day leave after extending In-Country, so I never got a chance to see Bob Hope.

IN-COUNTRY

"UP CLOSE" AT THE BOB HOPE SHOW.

Remembering my first R&R from Vietnam. I had been dealing with heat-rash for months, but by the second day in Singapore (and clean hot water) it went away.

IN-COUNTRY

YOU THOUGHT IT COULDN'T POSSIBLY GET ANY BETTER.

....I DON'T MIND BEING WRONG ONCE IN A WHILE!

Distasteful jobs require proper handling!

TACTICAL DELEGATION OF AUTHORITY.

IN-COUNTRY

TOO MUCH KNOWLEDGE CAN BE DANGEROUS!

IN-COUNTRY

IN-COUNTRY

LIFE BACK AT BASE CAMP...NO SWEAT!

IN-COUNTRY

Believe it or not, this actually happened in our unit!

I think every unit had at least one guy with a problem dealing with authority and/or discipline. The CO found our problem child was able to release his aggression by taking him to a location with huge trucks and dozers, and letting him drive around for an hour or two a week.

IN-COUNTRY

THE MIXED BLESSING!

I seem to remember during Tet 1968 it came out that our First Sergeant had traded our only 50 caliber machine gun for an air conditioner!

IN-COUNTRY

DON'T WORRY...WE'RE IN THIS TOGETHER!

IN-COUNTRY

Anyone who drove in Saigon can attest to the fact that on main arterials there were usually at least eight different lanes of military vehicles (big and small), animals, cyclos, motorcycles, cars, bikes, buses woven in an ever-changing random pattern! I remember hearing a pro race car driver on a USO tour (Andretti?) declined an offer to drive in Saigon.

IN-COUNTRY

IN-COUNTRY

VIETNAMESE "SWEATER GIRL!"

A lot of guys just couldn't help "gilding the lily"....just a little!

IN-COUNTRY

TECHNICALLY ACCURATE...I GUESS...

THE SPECIAL BOND BETWEEN DOG AND HANDLER.

Using clever cover and disguise "The Company" went about their business undetected!

IN-COUNTRY

THE LOW-PROFILE OF THE CIA IN VIETNAM!

I'm probably being a little harsh. At least the food was hot/warm... and not C-rats!

IN-COUNTRY

FEEL FREE TO ASK FOR SECONDS!

IN-COUNTRY

WHAT WE HAVE HERE, IS A FAILURE TO COMMUNICATE!

THE VIETNAMESE ABILITY TO ADAPT...DIVERSIFY.

IN-COUNTRY

THE MANDATORY EARLY WARNING DEVICE!

IN-COUNTRY

NOBODY LIKES BEING PROVEN WRONG!

IN-COUNTRY

REMEMBER TWO-WEEK MAIL DELIVERY FROM HOME?

Army Sick-Call could be pretty entertaining. Although this actually took place in Germany, I'm sure things like this (and worse) happened In-Country!

IN-COUNTRY

CHEW ON **THAT** FOR A WHILE!

IN-COUNTRY

I GET BY WITH A LITTLE HELP FROM MY FRIENDS!

IN-COUNTRY

THE HO CHI MINH.............TRAIL???

IN-COUNTRY

IN-COUNTRY

WELL OK......AS LONG AS I REALLY NEED THEM!

IN-COUNTRY

THE SHORT-TIMER'S RE-UP TALK.

Many guys earned (or were saddled with) nicknames. There were numerous men in our relatively small unit, whose first name I'm sure I never knew.

IN-COUNTRY

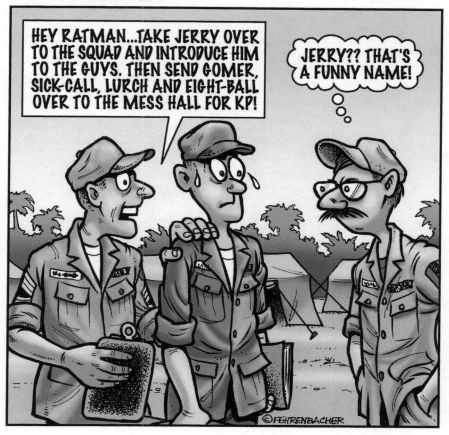

NICKNAMES? DON'T WORRY JERRY, YOU'LL GET YOURS!

Remembering that hills in your area of operation were referred to by their height in meters. "Hamburger Hill" was also called Hill 937.

IN-COUNTRY

I don't think I slept a wink the night before leaving Vietnam.

THE LAST NIGHT IN-COUNTRY JITTERS!"

ACHIEVING "SUCK-CESS" THROUGH TEAMWORK!

...AND THIS LITTLE "**PIG**gie" WENT TO WAR!

IN-COUNTRY

IN-COUNTRY

IN-COUNTRY

DO YA FEEL LUCKY...WELL, DO YA??

IN-COUNTRY

TAKE A WALK ON THE WILD SIDE!

I have to admit, I never experienced this, but heard from many of my friends...particularly when the sweat hit the cuts!

IN-COUNTRY

ELEPHANT GRASS - HAPPY TRAILS TO YOU....

IN-COUNTRY

JUST "POSING" FOR A PICTURE, SARGE!

Remembering how tough it was to be away from home in a hostile, extremely tropical environment during the holidays. The military did what it could to serve a hot turkey dinner when possible, but many still had to "make do!"

IN-COUNTRY

NOTHING LIKE BEING "HOME" FOR THE HOLIDAYS...
NOTHING!

Today's cartoon is a tribute to Chris Noel (apologies to Chris, I have trouble drawing good-looking women)! Can't imagine many veterans are unaware of her contribution to vets.

IN-COUNTRY

CHRIS NOEL...STILL SUPPORTING OUR TROOPS!

LEARNING THE LOCAL EXCHANGE RATE.

B-52 carpet bombing runs (like Operation Arc Light and Operation Rolling Thunder) were terrifying to the enemy. The planes flew so high "Charlie" didn't know they were there...until their world started coming apart.

IN-COUNTRY

'TIS BETTER TO GIVE THAN TO RECEIVE!

Merry Christmas everybody! (An explanation of where the producers of "A Christmas Story" got the idea for this famous line!)

IN-COUNTRY

A VIETNAMESE CHRISTMAS STORY!

When you first learn that "Pee tube" does not mean pneumatic!

IN-COUNTRY

HOW TO CURE A BASHFUL BLADDER!

The Republic of Korea (ROK) troops were extremely feared by Charlie, and according to many reports, the local civilians too. My Korean Tae Kwon Do instructor was with the White Horse Division. He told me that there was a waiting list for Korean soldiers wanting to serve in Vietnam. I'm not sure of the arrangement, but evidently the US paid or subsidized Koreans in SVN. SGT Lee told me he made more than a university professor in Seoul.
(BTW- I don't believe a Korean soldier would be quite this lenient!)

IN-COUNTRY

SUDDENLY, "CHARLIE" FOUND HIMSELF BETWEEN A ROCK AND...WELL...A ROK!

IN-COUNTRY

An unpleasant subject, but wanted to cover what everybody knew.

IN-COUNTRY

WAITING FOR "THE OFFICIAL" COUNT!

Made in the USA
Lexington, KY
10 April 2017